THE LAND OF JESUS

205 Colour illustrations

BONECHI & STEIMATZKY

ISBN 88-8029-990-5

© Copyright by Casa Editrice Bonechi
Via Cairoli 18/b - 50131 Florence - Italy
Tel. +39 055/576841 - Fax +39 055/5000766
e-mail: bonechi@bonechi.it - Internet: www.bonechi.it

Printed in Italy by Centro Stampa Editoriale Bonechi.

Text: Giuliano Valdes.

Translation: Rowena Hill of TRADUCO Snc - Florence

The photographs are the property of the Archives of the Casa Editrice Bonechi and were taken by:
Paolo Giambone, Garo Nalbandian *and* Alessandro Saragosa.
Photos on page 72: Zev Radovan.

The paintings shown on pages 4, 17, 22, 34, 37, 40, 46, 54, 62, 69 and 73 are: *The Annunciation of Cestello*, Botticelli (Uffizi); *The Baptism of Christ*, Verrocchio (Uffizi); *The Adoration of the Shepherds*, Luca Cambiaso (Pinacoteca of Brera); *The Adoration of the Shepherds*, Hugo Van der Goes (Uffizi); *The Slaughter of the Innocents*, Ludovico Mazzolino (Uffizi); *The Baptism of Christ*, Pseudo Boccaccino (Pinacoteca of Brera); *Marriage at Cana*, Andrea Boscoli (Uffizi); *St. Peter Walking on the Waters*, Alessandro Allori (Uffizi); *The Transfiguration*, Giovanni Girolamo Savoldo (Uffizi); *The Resurrection of Lazarus*, Palma il Vecchio (Uffizi); *Entry into Jerusalem*, Pietro Lorenzetti (Assisi, Lower Church).

INTRODUCTION

The land of Jesus, more usually known as the Holy Land, occupies a most prominent position in the geographical heart of the modern state of Israel. Naturally and historically a distinct region of the Middle East, the Holy Land faces the Mediterranean sea, and borders in the North on Lebanon, in the East on Syria and Jordan, and in the South on the Sinai desert. Always a meeting place and a bone of contention of many peoples, the Holy Land, at the threshold of the twenty-first century, is far from having achieved the state of serene and peaceful concord which would be appropriate to a region which for thousands of years has been a conduit for cultural and commercial influences from Europe, Asia and Africa.

From the geographical point of view, it is possible to identify in this region at least four quite different areas: the coastal plain along the Mediterranean; the mountains to the East of the plain, running South from the hilly region of Galilee and Samaria to that of Judea; the Negev, mostly arid desert, between Beersheba and the Gulf of Eilat; and the steep-sided valley between the mountains and the River Jordan (the Rift Valley). The landscape of the Holy Land is one of the most haunting and interesting in the world. Full of strident contrasts, it is at the same time permeated by an intense, sunny luminosity, which highlights its shades and colours, lending an extraordinary fascination to the harsh, bare, rocky, arid mountains, the lush, green oases, the fields and plantations, the great blue lake, the coastline trimmed with palms, and even to the deserts.

In this emotionally charged setting, the religious element plays an important part. This corner of the Middle East is a crossroads of the world's monotheistic religions, Christianity, Judaism and Islam, which find there their common religious matrix, as well as strange convergences, difficult to imagine. The Holy Land is, in fact, the setting for the life, activity, preaching, miracles and sacrifice of Jesus; but also the land of the great story of the Old Testament, historical heritage and document of the faith of a whole nation, as well as the place of the mystical ascent of Mohammed. The sites associated with Jesus; the visible signs of an extraordinary past; the vast archaeological remains; the imposing, varied and eclectic architecture; the turmoil of faith and the Holy Places, all invite the people of our time to deep reflection. And while the sinister gleams of never dormant strife continue to light up the scenery of the Holy Land, perpetuating the memory of ancient sacrifices first recorded in the books of the Bible, the many pilgrims who come there from every corner of the earth meditate on the meaning of the message of peace, faith, hope and universal good will that emanates from this strip of land. A visit to Israel cannot help becoming a sort of pilgrimage through the Holy Land, which is the essential core of this state.

The discovery of the Christian ambience, and visits to churches, basilicas, temples, the Western Wall, the Dome of the Rock and other manifestations of the Jewish and Islamic faiths, add up to an unusual experience. Tourists and visitors cannot remain indifferent before these elevated expressions of the cultural and religious heritage of a large portion of the human race.

NAZARETH

BASILICA OF THE ANNUNCIATION

"And in the sixth month the angel Gabriel was sent from God unto a city of Galilee, named Nazareth, To a virgin espoused to a man whose name was Joseph, of the house of David; and the virgin's name was Mary. And the angel came in unto her, and said, Hail thou that art highly favoured, the Lord is with thee: blessed art thou among women. And when she saw him, she was troubled at his saying, and cast in her mind what manner of salutation this should be. And the angel said unto her, Fear not, Mary: for thou hast found favour with God. And behold, thou shalt conceive in thy womb, and bring forth a son, and shalt call his name Jesus" (Luke, I 26-30).

Nazareth, spreading pleasantly over a green spur of the hills in lower Galilee and not far from the huge lake of Tiberias (also called the Sea of Galilee), is a small city of mostly modern appearance. Although the earliest human dwellings on the site date from the remote Aeneolithic age, the growth and urban development of the village that witnessed the childhood of Jesus, are of relatively recent origin. Not until the seventeenth century, when a Franciscan community settled there permanently, did favourable conditions exist for the place to be repopulated.

Nazareth: the facade of the Basilica of the Annunciation.

Nazareth: detail of the facade of the Basilica ▶ of the Annunciation.

Nazareth: view of the Crypt of the Basilica of the Annunciation and a detail of the dome.

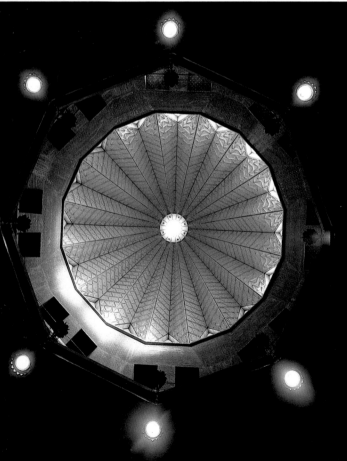

Nazareth: Basilica of the Annunciation, two views of the ▶ Grotto of the Virgin, believed to be the place where the Angel announced to the Virgin Mary that she was to become a mother.

Formerly, Nazareth had experienced a stormy history, conquered by the Romans and later by the Arabs, and only during the period of the Crusades (at the end of the eleventh century) had seen a time of splendour as the seat of bishops and the main administrative centre of Galilee. It was destroyed in the second half of the thirteenth century, and abandoned. The Nazareth of our days is a conglomerate of races and religions, whose observances require different kinds of buildings. Thus, beside the Jews and the Arab Muslims — who form the two numerically largest groups — smaller groups are also represented: Melchites and Greek Orthodox, Roman Catholics, Maronites, and other smaller Churches.

The most impressive architectural and artistic monument in the town is the **Basilica of the Annunciation**. The building, an imposing and dramatic landmark in the landscape of Nazareth, is of decidedly modern appearance, enhanced by the lofty dome. This dome, which rests on a poligonal tambour, is enriched at its base by a loggia; the roof is pyramidal and crowned by an architectural element in the shape of a lantern, above which rises the symbol of the Cross. The present church, built over a Crypt enclosing the Grotto of the Virgin, where the Archangel Gabriel announced to the Virgin that she would become mother, was completed in 1969 after the design by the Italian architect Giovanni Muzio. Before that, at

◄ *Nazareth: Basilica of the Annunciation, a view of the interior with the large mosaic representing the "Triumph of the Universal Church".*

Nazareth: Church of St. Joseph, a view of the Crypt built over the place where Joseph's carpenter's shop is believed to have stood.

the same sacred spot, five churches had risen in succession, starting in the year 365. In 1955 the last one, a Franciscan church, was dismantled to make way for the present basilica. According to well substantiated tradition, the first church was built by Helen, mother of the Emperor Constantine. This was, in fact, the first place in Galilee where Christianity was practised. Still in the fourth century, the Byzantines raised a new building, which was replaced by the Crusaders (twelfth century) with another church with an aisled nave. Finally, in the first half of the seventeenth century, it was the turn of the Franciscans, the guardians of the Christian Holy Places who erected the church which survived until the mid-fifties of our century.

The interior of the so-called *Upper Church* is remarkable for the daring and modernity of its architectural features, and encompasses a nave and aisles, divided by sturdy concrete pillars. Noteworthy is the chancel, dominated by an immense mosaic representing the *Triumph of the Universal Church*. Halfway up the nave is the entrance to the *Crypt* which houses the *Grotto of the Virgin*, with a pillar bearing the inscription "Ave Maria", to the eternal memory of the Gospel episode of the Annunciation, which according to tradition took place here.

CHURCH OF ST. JOSEPH

This sacred building is substantially modern in appearance. The architectural features of the outside of the church, known also as the *Church of the Holy Family*, obviously imitate the Romanesque style. This is particularly clear in the tripartite apse, in the succession of elegant small arches which adorn the high walls of the building, and in the sturdy, square belltower, made more airy by double and triple lancet windows.

The present church, which belongs to the Franciscans, is the result of the reconstruction, during the first quarter of our century, of a thirteenth century building. The fact that this older church was built over other ancient buildings which have revealed vestiges of baths and grottoes and the remains of further, even more ancient constructions, has given weight to the supposition that the carpentry workshop of Joseph was situated there. However, the convent of the Dames de Nazareth and that of St. Gabriel also claim to have the site of the workshop of Jesus' putative father; this is only one example of the numerous disputes over the exact location of the Gospel places in the Holy Land.

Nazareth: views of the picturesque and evocative alleys of the little town. These places, which are now enlivened by markets for all kinds of goods, must once have been the setting for the games of Jesus' childhood.

CHURCH OF ST. GABRIEL

Near the road to Tiberias is the interesting complex consisting of this church and **Mary's Well**. According to the version to be found in the apocryphal gospels, this well is the true place of the Annunciation; the Archangel Gabriel is said to have announced to Mary that she was to become a mother while she was going to the well to fetch water. The main spring of the well, which for twenty centuries has supplied Nazareth, is right under the *Crypt* of the Greek Orthodox church of St.Gabriel. This building, topped by a slim stone belltower, was completed in the middle of the eighteenth century.

In front of the church is a courtyard which is entered by a gate similar on the outside to a Roman arch, in a square, turreted structure. Inside the church a very fine *Iconostasis*, adorned with splendid icons, is preserved. Going through the *Crypt*, which is enriched with polychrome marble and refined ornaments based on geometrical motifs, it is possible to admire the main spring of Mary's Well, against the background of a construction of large stone blocks.

Nazareth: the Spring of the Virgin and a view of the turreted arch leading into the courtyard in front of the Church of St. Gabriel.

Nazareth: facade and bell-tower of the Church ▶ of St. Gabriel.

Nazareth: Church of St. Gabriel, a view of the splendid iconostasis and a detail of the ciborium above the altar.

Nazareth: Church of St. Gabriel, a view of the Crypt and ▶ the so-called Mary's Well, in fact the main spring of the Fountain of the Virgin.

EIN KAREM

CHURCH OF ST. JOHN THE BAPTIST

". . .There was a man sent from God, whose name was John. The same came for a witness, to bear witness of the Light, that all men might believe. He was not that Light, but was sent to bear witness of that Light" (John, I 6-8).

This picturesque hillside village, part of Jerusalem since 1961, is, in spite of its small size, quite important in the events narrated in the Gospels. Identified as the biblical *Ein Hakarem*, mentioned in the Old Testament, its name means "the spring in the vineyard".

Until 1948 it was an Arab village, and was then abandoned by the original population, to be resettled by Israeli immigrants over the following years. The village is famous in the Gospels for the episode of the Visitation of Mary to Elisabeth, her cousin: "And it came to pass that, when Elizabeth heard the salutation of Mary, the babe leaped in her womb; and Elisabeth was filled with the Holy Ghost: And she spake out with a loud voice, and said, Blessed art thou among women, and blessed is the fruit of thy womb. . . And Mary said, My soul doth magnify the Lord, And my spirit hath rejoiced in God my saviour" (Luke, I 41-42 and 46-47); and for the birth of

John the Baptist: "Now Elisabeth's full time came that she should be delivered; and she brought forth a son. . . And it came to pass that on the eighth day they came to circumcise the child; and they called him Zacharias, after the name of his father. And his mother answered and said, Not so; but he shall be called John" (Luke, I 57 and 59-60). The **Church of St.John the Baptist** belongs to the Franciscan monastery of the same name. The first church rose here in the fifth century, over the place traditionally held to be the home of Zacharias and Elisabeth. Enlarged by the Crusaders and later used by Arabs as a caravanserai and stable, the church was rebuilt and trasformed several times. The latest additions, carried out by the Franciscans, date from the second half of last century and from the thirties of this century. The most striking part of the pleasantly adorned interior is the *Crypt*, which houses the so-called **Grotto of the Benedictus**, considered to be the place where John the Baptist was born. A marble star beneath the altar bears a Latin inscription: "Hic precursor Domini natus est" (Here was born the precursor of the Lord).

◄ *Panorama of Ein Karem.*

Ein Karem: exterior of the Church of St. John the Baptist.

Ein Karem: Grotto of the Benedictus.

CHURCH OF THE VISITATION

This church, beautifully located on the slopes of a rocky hill and shaded by cypresses, is also known as the *Church of the Magnificat*, in commemoration of the answer Mary gave her cousin Elisabeth in the Gospel episode of the Visitation. Her hymn to the glory of the Lord is inscribed in forty-one languages on one wall of the church. The present basilica is a Franciscan church designed by the Italian architect Antonio Barluzzi and built between 1938 and 1955. The Franscian Order had acquired the land as early as the second half of the seventeenth century. The construction work revealed the remains of earlier, more ancient sacred buildings; in particular, vestiges of a church of the Byzantine era and of a similar building

Ein Karem: exterior of the Church of the Visitation and detail of the interior.

Ein Karem: Church of the Visitation, detail of the fresco ► representing ''The Meeting of Mary and Elisabeth'', and view of the well in the Crypt.

19

raised by the Crusaders in the twelfth century were found. In front of the Church of the Visitation, which is entered through an artistic wrought-iron gate, is a low portico topped by a graceful belltower. This building also consists of two parts. In the so-called *Upper Church* religious services are held, while in the *Crypt* is to be found a cave in which a miraculous spring broke forth at the exact moment when Elisabeth welcomed the Virgin. Among other curiosities, it is worth mentioning a stone against one wall which bears the imprint of a young boy's body. Traditionally, it is believed that this imprint was left by the infant John, when Elisabeth hid him from Herod's soldiers at the time of the slaughter of the Innocents.

Ein Karem: Church of the Visitation, remains of the ancient church built by the Crusaders and presbytery of the Upper Church.

Ein Karem: the artistic wrought-iron railings in front of the entrance to the Church of the Visitation, and the wall with the ''Magnificat'' written on it in forty-one languages.

BETHLEHEM

BASILICA OF THE NATIVITY

"And it came to pass in those days, that there went out a decree from Caesar Augustus, that all the world should be taxed. . . And Joseph also went up from Galilee, out of the city of Nazareth, into Judaea, unto the city of David, which is called Bethlehem; (because he was of the house and lineage of David:) To be taxed with Mary, his espoused wife, being great with child. And she brought forth her first-born son, and wrapped him in swaddling clothes, and laid him in a manger; because there was no room for them in the inn (Luke, II 1 and 4-7).

Not far South of Jerusalem lies the town of Bethlehem,

in the midst of a idyllic pastoral landscape, which has preserved almost unchanged the bucolic and biblical characteristics of remote times. It is a white town on the slope of a rough and rocky hill with patches of olive and cypress. From the sound, its name may mean either "the house of bread", from the Hebrew *Beit Lehem*, or "the house of meat", from the Arabic *Beit Lahm*. Bethlehem, a holy town for Christians, is permeated with reminiscences of both the Old and New Testaments. Still today, the vast tracts of pasture land are roamed by flocks of sheep and goats, led by shepherds who wear, now as in

Bethlehem: the outside of the Basilica of the Nativity has the appearance of a powerful fortified building.

Bethlehem: the Basilica of the Nativity is entered by way ▶ of the tiny Door of Humility.

Bethlehem: Basilica of the Nativity, view of the interior. The grandly monumental character of this church is emphasized by the rows of powerful red-sandstone Corinthian columns and by the fragments of ancient mosaic paving.

the past, severe dark robes and their typical headdress. Against this backdrop events transpired which are recorded in the Scriptures, both Jewish and Christian. The pastures known as the *"Shepherds' Fields"* witnessed lives of ancestors of David, the great king of the Jews; and they also witnessed the Angel's Annunciation of the birth of the Son of God to the Shepherds.

The birth of Jesus (form the Hebrew Jeshua) left an indelible imprint on the history of the human race. The story of the life of Christ on earth shows us a man whose twin nature, human and divine, left an immortal mes-

◄ Bethlehem: Basilica of the Nativity, view of the Altar of Christ's Birth.

Bethlehem: Basilica of the Nativity. A silver star, lit by fifteen lamps, marks the exact point where Jesus was born.

sage, which was handed down across the centuries and still today, two thousand years later, shapes a vast section of the conscience, the thought and the faith of the world. There is no agreement as to the exact date of Jesus' birth. Roman Catholics place it on the night of the 24th of December; the Greek Orthodox church believes the date was the 6th of January, and the Armenians place it as late as the 18th of January.

At this place revered by pilgrims since the first Christian centuries rises the **Basilica of the Nativity**. In 135 A.D. the emperor Hadrian, in his efforts to eradicate the Christian religion, dedicated the grotto and the little wood to the pagan god Adonis. Not until the intervention of Costantine, in 332, was it possible for Christians to pray in one of the places dearcst to Christian tradition; since then it has been a place of worship right up to our own times. An imposing basilica was built which was later completely destroyed, and a new church was erected

in the sixth century by Justinian, with the tripartite apse, the atrium transformed into a narthex, and two flights of stairs to allow access to the Grotto of the Nativity. It was spared by the Persian invaders in the seventh century; in the sixteenth century the Turks melted down the lead covering of the roof to make cannon-balls. The basilica, is surrounded by three monastery buildings belonging to different Christians Churches. Access to the basilica is by the very small *Door of Humility* (4 feet). Visitors thus must enter bending over, as if to a real cave. Originally, the door must have been far larger; it was reduced in size around the seventeenth century, so that the Muslims could not ride into the church on their horses. The interior is overwhelming, with the monumental grandness of the nave and four aisles, divided by four rows of powerful red limestone Corinthian columns, eleven to a row. Under some wooden boards can be glimpsed patches of the ancient mosaic floor. On the walls of the nave are

Bethlehem: Basilica of the Nativity, a view of the Grotto and a ceremony at the Altar of Christ's Birth.

◀ *Bethlehem: Basilica of the Nativity. In the Grotto of the same name stand the Altar of Christ's Birth and the Altar of the Manger; a detail of the latter can be seen below.*

traces of admirable mosaics on a gold ground, dating from the second half of the twelfth century and attributed to a certain *Basilius pictor*. The subjects depicted in the mosaic are the ancestors of Christ and the first seven Ecumenical Councils.

However, the part of this church with the greatest religious and historical significance remains the **Grotto of the Nativity**. This small chamber, partially lined with marble decorations, houses the *Altar of Christ's Birth*. A silver star lit by the light from fifteen silver lamps representing the different Christian communities marks the traditional place of Jesus's birth. The star bears a Latin inscription: "Hic de Virgine Maria Jesus Christus natus est — 1717". Two more altars face each other across the Grotto. The *Altar of the Manger* is the place where the Baby Jesus was laid after he was born. The clay manger, according to tradition found by St. Helen, was replaced by her with a silver manger. The *Altar of the Magi* stands at the place where the Magi paid homage to the newborn Son of God.

Bethlehem: Church of St. Catherine, view of the Cloister of the same name and the facade of the church with the statue of St. Jerome in front of it.

CHURCH AND CLOISTER OF ST. CATHERINE

There is a network of caves by way of which the Church of St. Catherine can be reached from the Grotto of the Nativity. This church was erected by the Franciscan order in the second half of the last century. The interior has an aisled nave and a cross-vaulted ceiling with ribs. The fame of this church rests on the solemn Roman Catholic midnight mass celebrated there at Christmas. The midnight mass is broadcast, by satellite, to TV networks all over the world.

The **Cloister** of the church is surprising for its composed,

Bethlehem: Interior of the Church of St. Catherine.
Opposite: View of the entrance to the so-called Milk Grotto.

evocative atmosphere. It is a small, serene space, made airier by the presence of palms and Mediterranean plants and by the graceful arrangement of the pretty twin columns which support the arches of the portico. In the centre of the Cloister, which dates from the time of the Crusades, rises a pillar with the sculptured figure of *St. Jerome*. According to tradition, this saint, who was known for his vast erudition and his knowledge of Latin, Greek, Hebrew and Aramaic, passed the last thirty-five years of his life, from 385 to 420, in one of the caves here. He worked there on the ''Vulgate'', the translation of the Bible into Latin.

◀ *The landscape of the hills round Bethlehem is still agricultural and pastoral in character.*

The houses of Bethlehem rise from an evocative landscape whose bare rocky slopes are dotted with occasional olive trees.

SHEPHERDS' FIELD

SANCTUARY OF THE SHEPHERDS

"And there were in the same country shepherds abiding in the field, keeping watch over their flock by night. And, lo, the angel of the Lord came upon them, and the glory of the Lord shone round about them: and they were sore afraid. And the angel said unto them, Fear not: for behold, I bring you good tidings of great joy, which shall be to all people. For unto you is born this day in the city of David a Saviour, which is Christ the Lord. And this shall be a sign unto you; Ye shall find the babe wrapped in swaddling clothes, lying in a manger" (Luke, II 8-12). The Sanctuary of the Shepherds has the appearance of a modern Christian church of admirable architectural design. It was built during the mid-fities of this century, and designed by the Italian architect Antonio Barluzzi, who has left numerous fine examples of his work all over the Holy Land. From the outside the building, which is crowned by a graceful little bell gable and a innovative wide-spanning cupola, is reminiscent in its essential lines of nomadic tents. The luminous interior is circular. A ring of low arches marks off the sanctum where the high altar stands, and supports the tambour of the cupola, which is decorated with angels. Three frescoes, painted in the early fifties, adorn the fifties, adorn the church, representing *The Birth of Jesus, The Shepherds Told by the Angel of Jesus' Birth, The Shepherds on the Way to Bethlehem.* The Sanctuary of the Shepherds, which stands at the edge of the so-called Shepherds' Field, near the village of Beit Sahour, occupies a place dear to both the Jewish and the Christian religions, since it is the site both of the biblical episode of Ruth and Boaz and of the gospel proclamation to the shepherds of the birth of Christ. There was a grotto at this place from very ancient times, which was already frequented by the earliest Christian communities. It shows fragments of mosaic floors of the fourth century. From the fifth century onwards the work of building a church and an upper chapel embellished with mosaics went forward. The chapel was demolished (sixth century) to make way for a basilica. Razed to the ground by the Persians in the first half of the seventh century, it was rebuilt in the shape of a fortified church, which in its turn became a monastery, and was then destroyed by the Egyptians in the tenth century. It was not until the beginning of the sixteenth century, and then by the efforts of the Greek Orthodox community, that the refashioning of the entire area was undertaken.

Shepherds' Field: exterior of the Sanctuary of the Shepherds.

*Shepherds' Field: Sanctuary of the Shepherds, detail of the ►
frescoes in the interior representing "The Birth of
Jesus", "The Shepherds on the Way to Bethelehem",
"The Shepherds Told by the Angel of Jesus' Birth".*

HERODION

HEROD'S FORTRESS

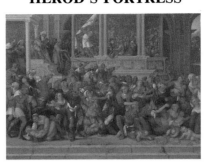

"And when they were departed, behold, the angel of the Lord appeareth to Joseph in a dream, saying, Arise, and take the young child and his mother, and flee into Egypt, and be thou there until I bring thee word: for Herod will seek the young child to destroy him" (Matthew, II 13).
Not far from Bethlehem, in the wild and arid setting of this part of Judea, rises the rough, conical hill dominated by the *Herodion*, a fortified palace built by Herod the Great. The powerful remains of this citadel, one of the most grandiose architectural projects realised by Herod, date from the second half of the first century B.C. From the top of the hill a desolate but impressive panorama can be enjoyed, sweeping across the Desert of Judea to the Dead Sea and including Bethlehem and Jerusalem. The palace became one of Herod's impregnable refuges, a true eagle's eyrie. The remains of walls and fortified towers, the fragments of mosaic, the great water cisterns, the buildings meant for baths and banqueting, are proofs of the magnificence of the original construction, which legend still holds to be the burial place of Herod.

◄ *Shepherds' Field: Sanctuary of the Shepherds, view of the Grotto of the Shepherds and the remains of a Byzantine building.*

Following pages: biblical associations and pastoral atmosphere in the landscape round the Shepherds' Field.

Herodion: ancient ruins facing the conical hill crowned by the remains of the fortress of Herod the Great.

YARDENIT

BAPTISM OF JESUS

Though not very important in ancient times from a strictly economic point of view, the river Jordan was of extraordinary religious and symbolic significance.

From the snowy summits of the Hermon, the Jordan runs almost 320 kilometres in twisting loops, in wider and narrower bends, at times impetuous and at times slow and placid.

This is the river that marks the boundary of the Promised Land; these are the waters that Moses was not allowed to cross. Joshua crossed them, and the event was solemnly recorded: "Hear, O Israel: Thou art to pass over Jordan this day ..." (Deuteronomy, 9, 1-3).

On these banks John the Baptist preached, and according to tradition Jesus was baptized there. The "Yardenit" Baptismal Centre was built by members of the nearby Kinneret kibbutz to receive the great numbers of pilgrims that go to the place; in these waters the Greek Orthodox and Catholic faithful symbolically renew their baptism. "Then cometh Jesus from Galilee to Jordan unto John, to be baptized of him. But John forbad him, saying, I have need to be baptized of thee, and comest thou to me? And Jesus answering said unto him, Suffer it to be so now: for thus it becometh us to fulfil all righteousness. Then he suffered him" (Matthew, III 13-15).

Yardenit: two views of the Jordan at this place, ▶ commonly believed to be where Jesus was baptized by John, with the river water, which is aspersed by Orthodox priests.

Desert of Judea: Jericho and its oasis seen across the desolate landscape of harsh, stony hills.

◄ *Desert of Judea: two pictures of the evocative natural landscape, enlivened by the presence of the green oasis of Jericho, which stands out beyond the remains of the ancient city (below).*

DESERT OF JUDEA

The vast area known as the Judean desert spreads South-East of Jerusalem down to the shores of the Dead Sea. The region also has a religious significance, since it recalls to mind episodes from the lives of Jesus and of John the Baptist. The word "desert" may not in itself be very attractive to tourists, but it has to be said that this desert exerts a great fascination. The desert places of Judea consist of endless sequences of rough and arid hills, deep-dug hollows and troughs and, at intervals, irregular ridges, all bearing the signs of erosion. This surreal, lunar landscape is certainly worth seeing.

JERICHO

The city of Jericho, situated not far from the banks of the Jordan in a fertile oasis dotted with palms and many other fruit trees, is one of the most ancient human settlements in the world. Archaeological studies carried out with the most modern sicentific istruments at the excavation site of Tel es Sultan, have made it possible to date the earliest settlements to 7800 B.C. The Jericho of our days, lying in a deep depression in the earth's surface, at about 250 metres below sea level, on the site of an ancient Byzantine town, is not more than a few kilometres away from the city described in the Bible and identified near the archaeological site of Tel es Sultan. There visitors can admire, together with other interesting vestiges of the past, a tower dating from the neolithic period. This is a most unusual example of fortifications in that prehistoric age. The Biblical city of Jericho, several times mentioned in the Scriptures, is universally known for the episode recounted in the Book of Joshua, when the Israelites brought down its impregnable walls with a mighty shout, after the priests' trumpets had sounded for seven days.

The bare rocky walls of the Mount of Temptation stand out against the green oasis of Jericho.

Mount of Temptation: rough terraces of rock surround ▶ the buildings and walls of a Greek Orthodox monastery.

MOUNT OF TEMPTATION

This harsh, bare mountain stands above the city of Jericho and the valley of the Jordan. The panoramic view from its summit sweeps from the green oasis of Jericho to the Jordan Valley to the Dead Sea, and to the vast mountainous region surrounding it. The Mount of Temptation is locally known as *Jebel Quruntul*, from "Quaranta"-forty, the number of days in the Gospel account of Christ's fast, when he withdrew into the wilderness after being baptised by John the Baptist in the nearby Jordan. The mountain, which from early Christian times has been called the Mount of Temptation, was referred to as "Mons Quarantana" by the Crusaders in the first half of the twelfth century.

The episode of the temptations of Jesus is thus described by Matthew (IV, 1-4 and 8-10): "Then was Jesus led up of the Spirit into the wilderness to be tempted of the devil. And when he had fasted forty days and forty nights, he was afterward an hungred. And when the tempter came to him, he said, If thou be the Son of God, command that these stones be made bread. But he answered and said, It is written, Man shall not live by bread alone, but by every word that proceedeth out of the mouth of God. . . Again, the devil taketh him up into an exceeding high mountain, and sheweth him all the kingdoms of the world, and the glory of them; And saith unto him, All these things will I give thee, if thou wilt fall down and worship me. Then saith Jesus unto him, Get thee hence, Satan: for it is written, Thou shalt worship the Lord thy God, and him only shalt thou serve".

Clearly visible on the side of the mountain are the walls and buildings of a Greek Orthodox monastery, built during the second half of last century on the site of an ancient paleo-Christian church. A grotto there has been made into a chapel, and is believed to be the place where Jesus fasted for forty days and forty nights.

CANA

CHURCH OF THE MIRACLE

"And the third day there was a marriage in Cana of Galilee; and the mother of Jesus was there: And both Jesus was called, and his disciples, to the marriage. And when they wanted wine, the mother of Jesus saith unto him, They have no wine. Jesus saith unto her, Woman, what have I to do with thee? mine hour is not yet come. His mother saith unto the servants, Whatsoever he saith unto you, do it" (John, II 1-5).

Thus begins the account of the Gospel episode according to John. The miracle of the marriage of Cana, where Jesus turns water into wine, constitutes a milestone in the Gospels, since it is the first miracle performed by Christ in the land of Galilee after his fast on the Mount of Temptation. Today there are at least three villages with the same name, but it is certain that the Cana described in the Gospel according to John can be identified as the village of *Kafr Kanna*, situated a little outside Nazareth on the road to Tiberias.

The setting of this village is an intensely evocative landscape, the features of which compose a truly tranquil and serene picture. Cana of Galilee provides a rare example of peaceful coexistence between different races and faiths. The village is inhabited by Greek-Orthodox and Roman Catholic Arabs and also by a Muslim minority, and a Jewish community existed here in Middle Ages. This fact shows up clearly in architectural details. A minaret and several domes stand out among the many little white houses, as if to make visible the peaceful diversity of the strands in the web of religion.

The **Church of the Franciscans**, known also as the *Church of the Miracle of Cana*, disputes with the Greek Orthodox church the honour of possessing the supposedly authentic waterjars used by the guests at the wedding feast recounted in the Gospel. This church, founded in the second half of last century, has a *Crypt*, built over the remains of ancient buildings, where a miraculous waterjar is kept. The facade of the church is flanked by twin belltowers, and topped by a characteristic red dome.

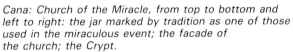

Cana: Church of the Miracle, from top to bottom and left to right: the jar marked by tradition as one of those used in the miraculous event; the facade of the church; the Crypt.

◄ Cana: Church of the Miracle, entrance to the Crypt.

Following pages: views of the Sea of Galilee with the Church of the Primacy of Peter.

Capernaum: views of the ancient ruins of a third- or fourth-century Synagogue.

CAPERNAUM

"And they went into Capernaum; and straightway on the sabbath day he entered into the synagogue, and taught" (Mark, I 21). "And thou, Capernaum, which art exalted unto heaven, shalt be brought down to hell: for if the mighty works, which have been done in thee, had been done in Sodom, it would have remained until this day. But I say unto you, That it shall be more tolerable for the land of Sodom in the day of judgment than for thee" (Matthew, XI 23-24).

The archaeological site of Capernaum is all that is left of an ancient city once extremely prosperous and important, especially in the period when Jesus was preaching. The Hebrew name of *Kefar Nahum* can be heard again today in common use, as the name of some very considerable ruins standing where the Jordan runs into the Sea of Galilee. An important road once passed (and still passes) there, by which the caravans made their way in Syria. Capernaum is mentioned many times in the Gospels. As well as the verses quoted above, there are accounts of several miracles performed by Jesus in that city, such as

the resurrection of the daughter of the alderman of the synagogue: "And he took the damsel by the hand, and said to her, Talitha cumi; which is, being interpreted, Damsel, I say unto thee, arise" (Mark, V 41); the healing of the centurion's servant (Luke, VII 1-10), and the chasing out of an unclean spirit from a man in the synagogue (Mark, I 23-26). In spite of the many miracles performed at Capernaum, as well as in other cities, the inhabitants were not converted, which provoked the bitter reproof of Christ, and especially the forecast of evil directed at Capernaum itself, quoted above.

The interesting remains of an ancient *Synagogue*, dating from the third or fourth century, are the most conspicuous landmark in the city, once splendid but fallen into decay and ruin with the irreversible damage done by earthquakes and warfare. It is almost possible to believe, on rereading the verses from Matthew's Gospel, that Jesus' prophesy has been exactly fulfilled. The synagogue, where we can admire the remains of the limestone walls, the pillars with their fine Corinthian capitals, and the decorated fragments of beams, has no connection with the synagogue where Christ used to teach, nor the one

Capernaum: the ruins of an ancient Byzantine church, supposed to have been once the House of Simon Peter, and other architectural remains.

Capernaum: among the ruins it is possible to distinguish the remains of an ancient mill, a Roman milestone, fragments of a mosaic and a broken pillar with a Corinthian capital.

built by the centurion whose servant was miraculously healed. It is believed that this one was built in the late imperial age, under the Emperor Julian, and is one of a series of similar religious buildings that arose in the upper part of Galilee with the financial support of the imperial authorities. This supposition appears to be confirmed in fact by the presence of decorative elements, such as gryphons, eagles, lions, dates, acanthus, seashells and others, which are usually prohibited in places destined for Jewish worship.

Not far from the synagogue can be seen the remains of an ancient building — in all probability a Byzantine church — which tradition holds to be the *House of Simon Peter*.

TABGHA

CHURCH OF THE LOAVES AND FISHES

"And when it was evening, his disciples came to him, saying, This is a desert place, and the time is now past; send the multitude away, that they may go into the village, and buy themselves victuals. But Jesus said unto them, They need not depart; give ye them to eat. And they said unto him, we have but five loaves, and two fishes. He said, Bring them hither to me. And he commanded the multitude to sit down on the grass, and took the five loaves, and the two fishes, and looking up to heaven, he blessed, and brake, and gave the loaves to his disciples, and the disciples to the multitude. And they did all eat, and were filled: and they took up of the fragments that remained twelve baskets full. And they that had eaten were about five thousand men, beside women and children" (Matthew, XIV 15-21). The place where this occurred, situated near the Sea of Galilee on the slopes of the Mount of Beatitudes, is known locally also as *Tabgha*. This name is the Arab version of a Greek word whose meaning seems from its sound to be "seven fountains" (*Heptapegon*). There are, in fact, some sulphurous springs in the area, once much prized and frequented because they cured skin diseases. According to tradition, it was by bathing in one of these springs that

Tabgha: Church of the Loaves and Fishes, a view of the mosaic symbolizing the well known miracle of Jesus.

Job was cured of leprosy. In our days the waters have been found to have a high level of radioactivity, so that their therapeutic use is not advised.

But the aspect of Tabgha which principally arouses the interest of visitors is the existence there of two churches commemorating two well-known episodes in the life of Jesus, the multiplication of the loaves and fishes and the third appearance to his disciples after the Resurrection.

The **Church of the Loaves and Fishes** is a modern building standing on the site of a fourth century Byzantine church, built where Jesus was sitting while he performed one of his best known miracles. The ancient church, already damaged by earthquakes in the sixth century, was completely destroyed a century later. All trace and even memory of it was lost, until Benedictine monks rediscovered, during last century, its very interesting vestiges. The interior of the basilica follows the classical pattern for this type of building: nave and aisles, transept, apse

Tabgha: Church of the Loaves and Fishes, views of the facade and the interior with its aisled nave.

Tabgha: Church of the Loaves and Fishes, the apse with the high altar and the artistic lamp, and one of the splendid floor mosaics.

and narthex. What makes this church one of the sights most frequently visited by tourists is the splendid mosaic decoration. Counted among the most refined examples of the art of mosaic in the Holy Land, the mosaics of the Church of the Multiplication of the Loaves and Fishes stand out for their vibrant colours and for the fine execution of decorative motifs, such as the animals and plants typical of the surroundings of the lake. But the most praised and best known mosaic is certainly the one which depicts symbolically the miracle after which the church is named: it shows a *basket full of loaves between two fishes*. Below the high altar is a stone marking the place where Christ put down the two fishes and five loaves.

Tabgha: The statue of a prophet looks down on the entrance to the Church of the Loaves and Fishes.

Tabgha: an ancient olive press.

Tabgha: Church of the Primacy of Peter, a detail of the sanctuary built on a great basalt rock and the monument commemorating the gospel episode.

Tabgha: Church of the Primacy of Peter, views of the exterior and the interior with the celebrated "Mensa Christi".

CHURCH OF THE PRIMACY OF PETER

This Christian temple rises near the shore of the lake with an evocative and picturesque landscape as its setting. The church was built by the Franciscans, in the early forties of this century, in dark blocks of basalt rock. From very ancient times there has been a rock there (it may now be seen inside the church) which was known by the Latin name of *Mensa Christi*. It is said that on that rock Jesus conferred on Peter the responsibility of being the future head of the Church. The Gospel story recounts on this subject how Christ appeared to his disciples for the third time after the Resurrection and how the primacy of Peter was then affirmed. "After these things Jesus shewed himself again to the disciples at the sea of Tiberias; . . . He saith unto him the third time, Simon, son of Jonas, lovest thou me? Peter was grieved because he said unto him the third time, Lovest thou me? And he said unto him, Lord, thou knowest all things; thou knowest that I love thee. Jesus saith unto him, Feed my sheep" (John, XXI 1 and 17).

MOUNT OF BEATITUDES

This improperly called "mount" is a hill standing above the Sea of Galilee, in a remarkably fine landscape. It is named after the Sermon on the Mount, during which Jesus proclaimed the Beatitudes to the crowd that had gathered to listen to him (Matthew, V 3-11).

The Church of the Beatitudes at the top of the hill was built in 1937 by the architect Antonio Barluzzi. This remarkable building is octagonal in structure. On the outside it is compassed by a colonnaded portico which runs right round the building. A bell gable stands in front of the dome, which is supported by an octagonal tambour. Inside, the eight windows each bear the text of the beginning of one of the Beatitudes enunciated by Jesus during the Sermon on the Mount.

Mount of Beatitudes: view of the hill with the church of the same name and a glimpse of the Sea of Galilee from the church porch.

Church of Beatitudes: from top to bottom and left to right: front view of the church; the high altar; the inside of the cupola. ▶

MOUNT TABOR

SANCTUARY OF THE TRANSFIGURATION

"And after six days Jesus taketh Peter, James, and John his brother, and bringeth them up into a high mountain apart. And was transfigured before them: and his face did shine as the sun, and his raiment was white as the light. And, behold, there appeared unto them Moses and Elijah talking with him" (Matthew, XVII 1-3).

The rounded shape of Mount Tabor dominates a vast region near Nazareth. Several times mentioned in the Old Testament, it is known among Christians for the Gospel story of the Transfiguration of Christ, which tradition places on Mount Tabor. Called by the Arabs *Djebel Tor*, or "mountain of the bull", it is associated with the practises of an ancient cult going back to the Canaanites. There are many references to this mountain in the Bible. It formed the boundary of the ter-

ritories ruled by the tribes of Zebulun, Issachar and Naphtali; it was there that Deborah forced Barak to collect ten thousand men to wage war against the king of Canaan, Jabin; and finally Hosea mentions the mountain when he is admonishing the leaders of Israel for their cult of idols and their corruption.

The modern **Basilica of the Transfiguration** (1923) commemorates the miraculous event recounted by Matthew. In front of the church are the remains of ancient churches. The facade of the Basilica is flanked byrs and is open in the centre where a great archway is supported by pillars. The interior, which is in three parts, has in the apse a modern mosaic representing the *Transfiguration*. The *Crypt* preserves architectural features from the period between the Byzantines and the Crusaders.

Mount Tabor: a panoramic view of the mountain and the beautiful facade of the Sanctuary of the Transfiguration.

Following pages: Sanctuary of the Transfiguration, views of the majestic interior of the basilica, the mosaic in the apse (the Transfiguration) and the Crypt.

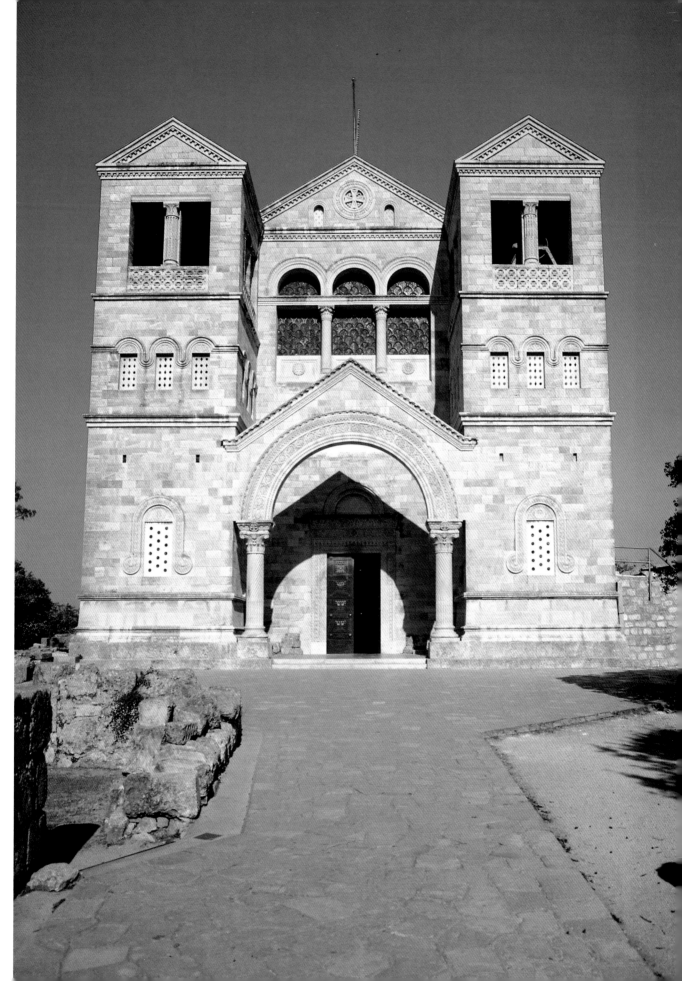

ET TRANSFIGURATUS EST ANTE EOS

The fortified entrance to the Sanctuary and the monument erected to commemorate the visit of Pope Paul VI (15-1-1964)

The backside of the Sancturary of the Transfiguration and the delightful view from the top of the mountain.

*Reflections of the setting sun illuminate
the Sea of Galilee.*

BETHANY

CHURCH AND TOMB OF LAZARUS

"Now Bethany was nigh unto Jerusalem, about fifteen furlongs off: And many of the Jews came to Martha and Mary, to comfort them concerning their brother. . . Then they took away the stone from the place where the dead was laid. And Jesus lifted up his eyes and said, Father, I thank thee that thou hast heard me. And I knew that thou hearest me always: but because of the people which stand by I said it, that they may believe that thou hast sent me. And when he had thus spoken, he cried with a loud voice, Lazarus, come forth. And he that was dead came forth, bound hand foot with graveclothes: and his face was bound about with a napkin. . ." (John, XI 18-19 and 41-44).

The ancient Bethany is the present day Arab village of El Azaryia, situated on the Eastern slope of the Mount of Olives, not far from Jerusalem. The present Arab place-name seems to derive from that of a Christian settlement of the Byzantine age: *Lazarion*. The historic name of "Bethany", by which the place is called in the Gospel according to St. John — while recounting the miracle of the resurrection of Lazarus and other events that happened there while Jesus was going from Jericho to Jerusalem — seems, on the other hand, to derive from *Beit Hanania*. It seems, in fact, that this was the name of the place at the time when it belonges to the tribe of Benjamin.

The **Church of Lazarus**, built over a grotto where visitors may see a chamber commonly known as the "Tomb of Lazarus", is a modern construction from the early fifties of our century.

Completed according to the design of the Italian architect Antonio Barluzzi, it is built in the form of a Greek Cross, crowned by a low dome supported on a poligonal tambour and flanked by a graceful belltower.

Bethany: Church of Lazarus, exterior.

DIXIT EI JESUS EGO SUM RESURRECTIO ET VITA

KINDLY SHOW RESPECT FOR THE SANCTITY OF THIS SITE

Bethany: the interior of the Church of Lazarus and entrance to the tomb.

Bethany: inside the Tomb of Lazarus.

This church is located in a quarter where other interesting buildings may be seen, such as a mosque crowned by a slim minaret, the ruins of a Benedictine monastery from the twelfth century and the new Greek Orthodox church. The present Church of Lazarus stands of the site once occupied by the ancient religious buildings which rose and fell there over the centuries. It is known that two oratories existed there during the Byzantine period, in the second half of the fifth century. Later, at the time of the Crusades, a new church rose, and the previous chapels eventually became part of it. Patches of mosaic paving are visible in the courtyard which belonged to previous buildings. The interior of the church resembles a mausoleum. The decorations in the lunettes, by G. Vagarini, represent *The Conversation of Martha and Mary with Jesus*, the *Feast of Bethany in the House of Simon the Leper* and *Jesus Resuscitating Lazarus*.
A stairway cut in the live limestone rock leads to an underground chamber; this is the so-called Tomb of Lazarus, the scene of one of the most acclaimed miracles performed by Jesus in the Holy Land.

JERUSALEM

THE LAST SEVEN DAYS

"On the next day much people that were come to the feast, when they heard that Jesus was coming to Jerusalem, Took branches of palm trees, and went forth to meet him, and cried, Hosanna: Blessed is the King of Israel that cometh in the name of the Lord. And Jesus, when he had found a young ass, sat there-on; as it is written, Fear not, daughter of Sion: behold thy King cometh, sitting on an ass's colt" (John, XII 12-15). Jerusalem: the name itself evokes an idea of universality and peace reaching beyond nationalisms, racial disputes, religious faiths and political barriers. In fact, the city that saw the earthly and historical end of Christ's story as told in the Gospels, is one of the main magnetic centres of the monotheistic religions of the world. Spreading pleasantly over the hills of Judea, it is the Holy City of humanity.

The place of the Passion and the Crucifixion of Jesus, it is the City of Peace, in spite of the invasions and pillagings that over the centuries have succeeded each other there, and that is what it is called by the Jews — Yerushalayim — *while the Arabs call it* El Kuds, *the Holy One.*

◄ *Manifestations of religion in Jerusalem.*

Jerusalem: an evocative panorama of the Holy City.

Jerusalem: a colourful crowd enlivens the picturesque market under the Damascus Gate.

Jerusalem: from top to bottom and from left to right: ▶ Herod's Gate, Lion Gate, Golden Gate, Zion Gate.

WALLS AND GATES

The magnificent walls that ring the city of Jerusalem, pierced by seven great and famous gates, are one of the most characteristic features of the Holy city. The pink stone walls, twenty meters high in places, run a length of almost four kilometers, enclosing the Old City. They were erected during the first half of the sixteenth century, after the conquest of the Holy Land by the Ottoman Turks. At the entrance from the ancient road leading North is the exquisite **Damascus Gate**. Recent archaeological exploration has revealed vestiges of the gate from the Roman times. **Herod's Gate**, called also the *Gate of Flowers*, leads to the Muslim quarter. Facing the Mount of Olives is the **Lion Gate**, or *St. Stephen's Gate*, so

called by Christians who believed it was the place of the martyrdom of that saint. The **Golden Gate**, known also as the *Gate of Mercy*, was walled up by the Muslims. It is supposed to have been built in the Byzantine period, and its foundations are said to date from as far back as the age of Solomon. The area of the *Wailing Wall* is reached by way of the **Dung Gate**, the strange name of which is related to the fact that, in Byzantine times, Christians used to throw their refuse among the ruins of the temple esplanade. The Jewish quarter is reached through the **Zion Gate**. The Arabs usually call it the *Gate of the Prophet David*, since it faces Mount Zion, which is supposed to be the burial place of David. The lively **Jaffa Gate** leads to the main road toward the West, and is named after the ancient Philistine port. The last is the **New Gate**, which was opened during the last century.

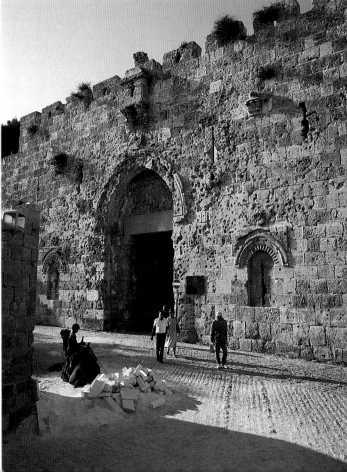

Jerusalem: Church of St. Anne, exterior with the ruins of the Pool of Bethesda, and a view of the Crypt, believed to be the place where the Virgin was born.

Jerusalem: two views of the ancient remains of the ▶ Pool of Bethesda.

CHURCH OF ST. ANNE AND POOL OF BETHESDA

This church, erected during the first half of the twelfth century, blends admirably traditional Romanesque features and the architectural principles followed at the time of the Crusades. It is numbered among the longest preserved sacred places in the city, since according to tradition it arose over the place where once stood the house of Joachim and Anne, the parents of the Virgin, who is supposed to have been born here. The interior has an aisled nave and exquisite capitals on the pillars sustaining the arches of the vault. A stairway leads down to the *Crypt*, held to be the birthplace of the Virgin.

The Pool of Bethesda is very close to the Church of St. Anne, near the Lions Gate. The imposing remains of a pool with two baths and five porches confirm the story told in the Gospel according to John. There was once a gate there called the Sheep Gate, near where a sheep market was held, and animals to be used in the city's sacrifices were washed in the pool. In this place Jesus performed the healing of a cripple (John, V 1-9).

CHURCH OF DOMINUS FLEVIT

This Franciscan church was built during the thirties of this century by the architect Antonio Barluzzi on the site of the remains of a fifth century building. In recent times the vestiges of a necropolis have been found nearby with funeral inscriptions in Greek, Hebrew and Aramaic. The window over the altar offers an incomparable panorama of Jerusalem. The name of the church is taken from the Gospel account of Christ weeping before the city unaware of its fate. ". . . And they shall not leave in thee one stone upon another; because thou knowest not the time of thy visitation" (Luke, XIX 44).

POOL OF SILOAM

This pool is one of the most important of the waterworks of ancient Jerusalem. It is attributed to King Hezechiah, who completed it toward the end of the eight century B.C., diverting through a tunnel the waters from the *Gihon Spring*. The place is known in the Gospels for the episode of the healing of the blind man. "He answered and said, A man that is called Jesus made clay, and anointed mine eyes, and said unto me, Go to the pool of Siloam, and wash: and I went and washed, and I received sight" (John, IX 11).

COENACULUM

This hall from the time of the Crusades is characterized by graceful ogival arches which span the stretch of the ribbed cross vault. In the fifteenth century, the Muslims took control of Mount Zion, turned the church into a mosque, and for more than five centuries forebade Jews and Christians access to it. This place, sacred in Christian tradition, is believed to be the site of the Last Supper where Christ established the rite of the Eucharist. In the same place, seven weeks later, the Holy Ghost appeared to Mary and the Apostles at the Pentecost.

MACCABEE STEPS

A very ancient flight of stone steps can be seen in the garden of the Church of St. Peter in Gallicantu. Its name refers to the period when it was built, in order to connect the city of David and the Valley of Kidron with Mount Zion above. The steps were certainly in use at the time when the events narrated in the Gospels were taking place. Jesus probably descended them on the evening of Holy Thursday, when he went to pray in Gethsemane.

◄ *Jerusalem: Church of St. Peter in Gallicantu and architectural rock tombs in the Valley of the Kidron.*

Jerusalem: panorama of Gethsemane with the Church of All Nations, dominated by the cupolas of the Russian Church of St. Mary Magdalene.

CHURCH OF ST. PETER IN GALLICANTU

This church, plesantly modern in appearance, was constructed in the thirties of this century for the Assumptionist Fathers. It is very probable that the house of the high priest Caiaphas once stood on this site, even if no support for this belief has been found by archaeological explorations, which, however, have revealed the remains of an ancient Byzantine basilica. The curious name of the church recalls the denial of Peter, as recounted in the Gospels: "Then began he to curse and to swear, saying, I know not the man. and immediately the cock crew. And Peter remembered the word of Jesus, which said unto him, Before the cock crow, thou shalt deny me thrice. And he went out, and wept bitterly" (Matthew, XXVI 74-75).

VALLEY OF THE KIDRON

This valley lies between the Old City of Jerusalem and the Mount of Olives, and offers the visitor a strange, rough landscape, characterized by the bare, stony hills dotted by a few olive trees and sparse bushes. It was the site of some episodes narrated in the Gospels, and is interesting particularly for the presence of several rock tombs of an architectural type which, although they are falsely called *Tombs of the Prophets*, unmistakably reveals their Hellenistic origin. The tomb known as the **Pillar of Absalom**, with its cone-shaped roof, the **Tomb of Jehoshaphat**, that of **Zacharias**, in the shape of a pyramid, and that of **St. James** should also be mentioned.

GETHSEMANE

The garden of Gethsemane is one of the sacred places dearest to Christian tradition. The fact that it is still rich today in olive trees hundreds of years old, twisted and gnarled, has confirmed the belief that these may be the very same olive trees that witnessed Jesus' last night before his arrest. The word "Gethsemane" originates from the Hebrew expression *Gat Shemen*, which means "olive press", in obvious reference to the natural abundance of these trees. Gethsemane holds an important place in the Gospel story, since Jesus spent there the night before his arrest, praying in mortal anguish: "And they came to a place which was named Gethsemane: and he saith to his disciples, Sit ye here, while I shall pray" (Matthew, XXVI 36).

Jerusalem: Gethsemane, the Olive Orchard.

Jerusalem: Gethsemane, the elegant classical facade of the modern Church of All Nations.

CHURCH OF ALL NATIONS

In the idyllic setting of Gethsemane, one of the most evocative sights in all Jerusalem, rises this church, built by the Italian architect Antonio Barluzzi between 1919 and 1924. The church, known also as the *Basilica of the Agony*, in reference to the night that Christ spent there on the eve of his Passion, blends the architectural lines typical of the Christian basilica (the facade) with the salient features of Islamic buildings (sides, and roof with numerous small domes). The name "Church of All Nations" commemorates the contributions made by many countries to its construction. The flags of the nations are represented inside the little domes which give the whole a distinctly oriental tone. On the site of the present church there rose first a fourth century Byzantine church, later transformed by the Crusaders into a basilica.

The facade, enclosed by an elegant wrought iron fence, stands at the top of a flight of steps. A mass of pillars supports the great arches surrounding the atrium, while the tympanum is adorned with a modern mosaic representing *Jesus as the Link between God and the Human Race*. Inside, some remnants of the mosaic paving document the existence of the ancient Byzantine church. The presbytery is the part of the church which most attracts the attention, since a large fragment of the rock on which Jesus is supposed to have prayed the night before the Passion can be seen in front of the high altar. The rock is entirely surrounded by a crown of thorns in wrought iron. In the lunette in the apse is a mosaic representing *Christ in Agony being Consoled by an Angel*. In the side apses are other mosaic representations of episodes in Jesus' passion, such as the *Kiss of Judas* and the *Arrest of Jesus*.

◄ *Jerusalem: Church of All Nations, view of the presbytery with the great mosaic in the apse representing "Christ in Agony being Consoled by an Angel".*

Jerusalem: Church of All Nations; the mosaics in the side apses represent "The Kiss of Judas" and "The Arrest of Jesus".

Jerusalem: Church of the Tomb of the Virgin, views of the facade and the Crypt, believed to be the place where the Virgin Mary was buried.

Jerusalem: Church of the Tomb of the Virgin, the tombs of the Virgin and St. Joseph.

Jerusalem: Russian Monastery, Armenian Chapel and mosaic paving.

CHURCH OF THE TOMB OF THE VIRGIN

Known also as the Church of the Assumption, this church has the form given to it by a reconstruction carried out by the Crusaders in the eleventh century. It is supposed, however, to have originated in the Byzantine period (fifth century), and the *Crypt* cut into the live rock, the most important part of the church from the touristic or religious point of view, is supposed to date from that time.

The tombs of Mary's parents, Anne and Joachim, and of her husband Joseph, are inside the church. A stairway leads down into the underground burial chamber where the so-called **Tomb of the Virgin** can be seen. It stands in the centre of the crypt, which is adorned with paintings, valuable icons and fine lamps. Although this church is claimed to be the tomb of Mary, it should be mentioned that another tomb of the Virgin is venerated in Ephesus, in Turkey, where the mother of Jesus is supposed to have been taken by the Apostle John and later died.

Jerusalem: Grotto of Gethsemane. This highly evocative place is where Jesus was arrested.

GROTTO OF GETHSEMANE

This grotto, which is not far from the Church of the Tomb of the Virgin, is supposed to be the place where Jesus, betrayed by Judas, was arrested. In spite of some renovations carried out in the late fifties of this century, of all the many holy places in Jerusalem the Grotto of Gethsemane has conserved best its original appearance,

that is, the appearance it had at the time of Christ's life on earth. Previously used by farmers to store grains, from the sixth century on it served some Christian communities as a cenacle.

Inside the cave, which has an impressive stone vault, are three altars with murals over them. Over the high altar is a representation of *Jesus Praying among the Apostles*, while the paintings over the side altars depict the *Assumption of the Virgin* and the *Kiss of Judas*.

VIA DOLOROSA

"And as they led him away, they laid hold upon one Simon, a Cyrenian, coming out of the country, and on him they laid the cross, that he might bear it after Jesus. And there followed him a great company of people, and of women, which also bewailed and lamented him. But Jesus turning unto them said, Daughters of Jerusalem, weep not for me, but weep for yourselves and for your children" (Luke, XXIII, 26-28).

The name of "Via Dolorosa" (or "*Via Crucis*") is relatively recent; it dates from the sixteenth century, when a name was sought for the stretch of road, between the fortress Antonia and Golgotha, along which Christ walked bowed under the weight of the Cross. The present route, however, is somewhat different from the one Jesus walked. Of the fortress Antonia, for example, where Christ was judged before Pilate and where Herod the Great had his residence, only a few scraps of paving remain. This building, which stood near the North-West corner of the Temple, was the starting-point for Jesus' painful walk toward Calvary, which at that time was outside the walls of the city. Every Friday afternoon the Franciscans lead a pious procession winding through the streets that witnessed Christ's suffering.

Jerusalem: Prison of Christ. Along the Via Dolorosa are several underground rooms in the shape of cells. According to an ancient tradition, Jesus was kept a prisoner in one of these; another theory identifies it as the place where Barabbas was gaoled.

Jerusalem: views of the facade of the Church of the Flagellation and its interior with the artistic stained-glass windows.

Jerusalem: Via Dolorosa, the Roman Arch of Ecce Homo rises at the second Station of the Cross.

I Station

The First Station is near the Monastery of the Flagellation, where Jesus was questioned by Pilate and then condemned. "Then Pilate therefore took Jesus, and scourged him. And the soldiers platted a crown of thorns, and put it on his head, and they put on him a purple robe, And said, Hail, King of the Jews! and they smote him with their hands" (John, XIX 1-3). The chapel, built during the 1920s on the site of a previous building erected by the Crusaders, is now run by the Franciscans, who set out from there each Friday for the traditional procession. The church possesses admirable stained-glass windows representing *Christ Scourged at the Pillar*, *Pilate Washing his Hands*, and the *Freeing of Barabbas*. Above the high altar, under the central dome, is a mosaic on a golden ground showing the *Crown of Thorns Pierced by Stars*.

II Station

The Second Station is near the remains of an ancient Roman construction known as the **Arch of Ecce Homo**, in memory of the words pronounced by Pilate as he showed Jesus to the crowd. Only part of this triumphal arch, erected under Hadrian (135 A.D.) to celebrate the capture of Jerusalem, is visible nowadays. The left arch, which no longer exists, formed at one time part of a monastery of Islamic dervishes; while the right arch is still preserved today inside the **Church of the Sisters of Zion**. This church was built during the second half of last century on a site which has yielded the remains of ancient ruins, such as the already mentioned Roman arch, part of the fortifications and courtyard of the fortress Antonia and remarkable vestiges of the Roman-age street paving, the so-called *Lithostratus*. On some of the stones are the signs of an ancient dice game, which has given support to the hypothesis that this was the place where the Roman soldiers gambled for Jesus' clothes. Mention should be made, finally, of the **Struthion Pool**, an ancient water reservoir from the second century B.C., later roofed over by the Emperor Hadrian.

Jerusalem: a view of the Via Dolorosa, and the marks for the game of dice engraved in the floor of the Church of the Sisters of Zion.

Jerusalem: a view of the Lithostratus, the ancient Roman ► *paving. It was at this point that Jesus took up the cross after being judged before Pilate.*

III Station

The Third Station commemorates Chirst's first fall on the Via Dolorosa. The place is marked by a small chapel belonging to the Armenian Catholic Patriarchate. It is a nineteenth century building renoveted and completed by Catholic soldiers of the Free Polish Army during World War II.

IV Station

The meeting between Jesus and his mother is commemorated by a small oratory with an exquisite lunette over the entrance, adorned by a bas-relief carved by the Polish artist Zieliensky.

V Station

An inscription on the architrave of one door recalls the encounter between Jesus and Simon the Cyrenian, who was given Christ's heavy Cross to carry to Golgotha, the place of the Crucifixion. This episode is confirmed by the Gospels, except that of John.

Jerusalem: Via Dolorosa, from top to bottom and left to right: the Third, Fourth and Fifth Stations of the Cross.

Jerusalem: Via Dolorosa. The narrow alleys now feature ▶ craftsmen's workshops and buildings of pure medieval type.

Jerusalem: Via Dolorosa. The Sixth Station of the Cross is marked by a Greek Catholic chapel.

Jerusalem: Via Dolorosa, the Seventh Station of the Cross.

VI Station

A church belonging to the Greek Catholics preserves the memory of the meeting between Jesus and Veronica, whose tomb may also be seen here. The holy relic of this meeting, during which, according to tradition, Veronica wiped Christ's face with a silk veil on which his features remained imprinted, has been kept, since the eighth century, in the Basilica of St. Peter in Rome.

VII Station

The place of Jesus' second fall is marked by a pillar, which rises at the crossroads between the Via Dolorosa and the picturesque and lively Market Street.

Jerusalem: The Eighth Station of the Cross is marked by this small time-blackened cross carved in the wall.

Jerusalem: view of the Via Dolorosa.

VIII Station

On the outer wall of a Greek Orthodox monastery is carved a small Cross blackened by time. It was at that point that Jesus met the pious women. This episode, recounted in the Gospel according to St. Luke, is quoted at the beginning of the chapter.

IX Station

The third fall of Jesus is commemorated by a column of the Roman period at the entrance to · the Coptic monastery. The last five Stations of the Cross are situated inside the Holy Sepulchre.

Jerusalem: interior of the Coptic Monastery. A Roman pillar near the entrance marks the place of the Ninth Station of the Cross.

Jerusalem: an evocative view of the belltower of the Holy Sepulchre and its domes.

HOLY SEPULCHRE

This is one of the most imposing churches in Jerusalem, and at first sight reveals the unmistakable features of Crusader architecture, plus a sort of mixture between the Norman and Arab styles. It is, without a doubt, one of the sights that visitors to the Holy City cannot miss, a magnetic centre where many religious orders and sects congregate and bear forceful witness to the Christian faith, a place sacred to the civic and religious awareness of Christendom, irrespective of ethnic, racial or religious divisions.

The place of the present church was once a quarry and the site of executions, and was therefore situated outside the city walls. The name "Golgotha", from the Hebrew *gulgoleth*, means "the skull", and refers to the strange appearance of the hill which may have recalled a human skull, and to the legend which identifies the hill as the burial place of the skull of Adam. ". . . And they took Jesus, and led him away. And he bearing his cross went forth into a place called the place of a skull, which is called in the Hebrew Golgotha" (John, XIX 16-17). In 135 A.D. the Emperor Hadrian had built on the hill where Christ's sepulchre stood the Forum and Capitol of the Aelia Capitolina sacred to the cult of Jupiter, Juno and Venus. The excavations performed in 325 by Helen, mother of Constantine the Great, brought to light again the place of Jesus' burial and the cross used to crucify Christ. When Constantine's basilica was built, beginning in 326 and finishing in 335, it left intact the rock of Golgotha, where a cross crowned by a ciborium was placed, and the rock with the cave of Christ's tomb. This rock tomb was surmounted by a round dome of considerable size called *Anastasis* (Resurrection). The basilica, which has four aisles besides the nave and a crypt, was razed to the ground by the Persians in 614. Fifteen years later it was rebuilt, and lasted untill 1009, when it was again destroyed, this time by the caliph El Hakem of Egypt. The Crusaders, who had conquered Jerusalem in 1099, enlarged and enriched the building, which had already been rebuilt in the meantime by the emperor Constantine Monomachus. Seriously damaged by fire in 1808, it was restored by the Greek Orthodox Church which considerably altered the original Latin design. At present, the Holy Sepulchre is shared by the Roman Catholic, Greek Orthodox, Armenian, Coptic, Syrian and Ethiopian communities.

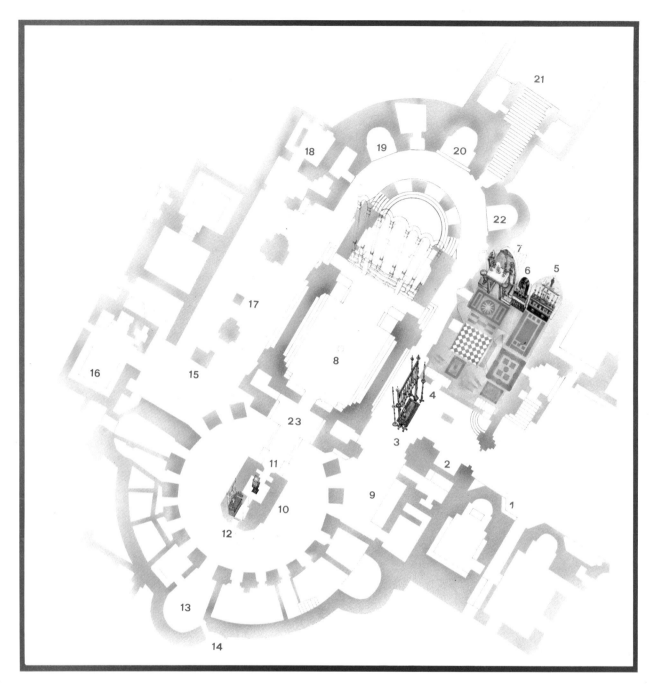

THE HOLY SEPULCHRE

1 - Entrance hall
2 - Muslims guards
3 - Stone of the Unction
4 - Chapel of Adam
5 - Altar of the Nails of the Cross
6 - Altar of Stabat Mater
7 - Altar of the Crucifixion
8 - Catholicon
9 - Place of Mourning
10 - Rotunda
11 - Sepulchre of Christ
12 - Coptic Chapel
13 - Jacobite Chapel
14 - Tomb of Joseph of Arimathea
15 - Altar of Mary Magdalene
16 - Franciscan Church
17 - Arches of the Virgin Mary
18 - Holy Prison
19 - Chapel of Longinus
20 - Chapel of the Division of the Holy Robes
21 - Chapel of Saint Helena
22 - Chapel of Derision
23 - Latin Choir

Jerusalem: The splendid facade of ► the Church of the Holy Sepulchre is flanked by a powerful belltower.

Jerusalem: Holy Sepulchre, a view of the Stone of the Anointing inside the great basilica and a detail of it.

Facing page: Holy Sepulchre, Altar of the Nails of the Holy Cross, which stands at the place of Golgotha.

Stone of the Anointing

In the entrance to the church of the Holy Sepulchre lies this long slab of polished pink limestone. Surrounded by candlesticks and lit by eight lamps, the stone marks the place of the ancient Oratory of the Anointing, which was demolished during the many architectural alterations to the building. According to tradition this is the place where Jesus' body was anointed after it had been taken down from the Cross, and where his Mother wept over him (Thirteenth Station). "And there came also Nicodemus, which at the first came to Jesus by night, and brought a mixture of myrrh and aloes, about an hundred pound weight. Then they took the body of Jesus, and wound it in linen clothes with the spices, as the manner of the Jews is to bury" (John, XIX 39-40).

Jerusalem: Holy Sepulchre, two views of the chapel of the Crucifixion with the life-size icons.

Jerusalem: Holy Sepulchre, the small Altar of the ▶ Stabat Mater.

Golgotha

"And when they were come to the place, which is called Calvary, there they crucified him, and the malefactors. . . Then said Jesus, Father, forgive them; for they know not what they do. . ." (Luke, XXIII 33 and 34). The place of the Crucifixion of Christ is taken today by two chapels, separated by the so-called *Altar of the Stabat Mater*, which recalls the grief of Mary at the moment of Christ's Deposition from the Cross. The first chapel, which is Roman Catholic, houses the so-called *Altar of the Nails of the Holy Cross*. There is a mosaic representing *Jesus being Stripped of his Raiment* (Tenth

Station) and *Jesus being Nailed to the Cross* (Eleventh Station). The second chapel, which is Greek Orthodox, is adorned with admirable life-size icons representing *Christ, the Virgin and St. John*. Below the image of the crucified Christ, hanging inert from the Cross, a rock can be seen where a silver ring marks the place where the Cross was fixed (Twelfth Station).

Christs' Sepulchre

The Shrine of the Holy Sepulchre (fourteenth and last Station of the Cross), placed in the middle of the rotunda of *Anastasis*, is the result of the transformation over centuries of an ancient Jewish tomb. The entrance leads into a first, larger chamber, known as the *Chapel of the Angel*. A fragment of rock marks the exact spot where the angel is supposed to have sat as he announced the Resurrection to the women. "And entering into the sepulchre, they saw a young man sitting on the right side, clothed in a long white garment; and they were affrighted" (Mark, XVI 5).

The mortuary chamber itself, of the type with niches, is small but evocative and full of symbols with intense emotional impact. This confined, candle-lit space is, in fact, the last Station of the Via Crucis, and is the place where the story of Christ's earthly life ended, until his glorious Resurrection, as the holy scriptures had foretold. A marble slab protects the rock of the tomb. Over the tomb can be seen a great number of silver lamps, which belong to four different Christian Churches. The three over the slab represent the *Resurrection* according to the Greek, Latin and Armenian versions.

Jerusalem: view of the Shrine of the Holy Sepulchre and the Chapel of the Angel.

Jerusalem: Holy Sepulchre; a small but evocative room guards the stone slab of Christ's tomb.

Jerusalem: Holy Sepulchre: two views of the stone slab of Christ's tomb.

Jerusalem: Holy Sepulchre, the splendid Iconostasis of the Katholikon and the admirable cupola above the crossing.

Katholikon

This is the central core of the imposing basilica, divided into two parts by a magnificent *Iconostasis* which rises from a short flight of steps. Above the crossing of the transept rises a great cupola called "of the *Omphalos*" (from the Greek word for "navel"), which is considered according to Christian tradition "the navel of the world".

Jerusalem: Holy Sepulchre, the interior of the Prison of Christ and the Chapel of Adam.

Holy Prison

Known also as the *Prison of Christ*, this is a narrow chamber which was once part of the more ancient buildings which stood on this site. The name, which came into common use in the seventh century, refers to the night that Jesus spent as a prisoner after his arrest at Gethsemane. On the other hand, there is a widely held opinion that this chamber is a visible vestige of an ancient prison annexed to the Forum of the Aelia Capitolina.

Crypt of St. Helen

This crypt, which has an impressive underground setting, is called after the mother of the Emperor Constantine the Great, and recalls the immense labour undertaken by him for the revival of the Holy Places, leading to the discovery of the cross and Jesus' tomb. The crypt has a dome from the age of the Crusades (twelfth century), supported by four pillars from the eleventh century. The chapel belongs to the Armenian Church.

Jerusalem: Holy Sepulchre, an evocative view of the Crypt of St. Helen and the so-called Tomb of Joseph of Arimathea.

Tomb of Joseph of Arimathea

This small chamber, dug in the live rock with some partial traces of masonry, is the only part inside the Holy Sepulchre which belongs to the Ethiopian Church. It seems truly to be an ancient Jewish tomb situated in the vicinity of Christ's sepulchre. The name of the tomb refers to Joseph of Arimathea, the owner of the rock tomb where Jesus was buried. ''And now when the even was come, because it was the preparation, that is, the day before the sabbath, Joseph of Arimathea, an honourable counsellor, which also waited for the kingdom of God, came, and went in boldly unto Pilate, and craved the body of Jesus. . . And he bought fine linen, and took him down, and wrapped him in the linen, and laid him in a sepulchre which was hewn out of a rock, and rolled a stone unto the door of the sepulchre'' (Mark, XV 42-43 and 46).

TOMB OF THE GARDEN

This tomb, probably from the Byzantine period, is situated outside the walls, to the North of the Damascus Gate, and is believed by many Christians, but specially the Protestants, to be the true burial place of Christ. This possibility seems to be indirectly confirmed in the Gospel: "Now in the place where he was crucified there was a garden; and in the garden a new sepulchre, where was never man yet laid. There laid they Jesus therefore because of the Jews' preparation day; for the sepulchre was nigh at hand" (John, XIX 41-42). The tomb is known also as *Gordon's Calvary*, after Charles Gordon, the British general who discovered the place in 1883 while he was admiring the strange landscape of Golgotha.

CHAPEL OF THE ASCENSION

This admirable building blends the architectural features of the Crusader style with traits belonging to the Muslim tradition. The chapel rises on the site of an ancient paleo-Christian sanctuary, near the top of the Mount of Olives. The original building was surrounded by a double portico forming a circle. Destroyed by the Persians in the 614, it was rebuilt by the Crusaders in the form of a small, octagonal temple (twelfth century). Having come under the control of the Muslims, to whom it has belonged since the thirteenth century, the building was converted into a mosque and completely transformed by walling in the arches and roofing over the octagon with a little dome of evident Islamic character. On a rock inside can be seen a footprint which is identified according to Christian tradition as the print that Jesus left as he ascended to Heaven: "And he led them out as far as to Bethany, and he lifted up his hands, and blessed them. And it came to pass, while he blessed them, he was parted from them, and carried up into heaven" (Luke, XXIV 50-51).

◄ *Jerusalem: view of the Tomb of the Garden, known also as Gordon's Calvary.*

◄ *Jerusalem: the ancient walls near the Tomb of the Garden.*

Jerusalem: Chapel of the Ascension, exterior and rock with the imprint of Jesus' foot.

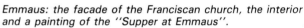
Emmaus: the facade of the Franciscan church, the interior and a painting of the "Supper at Emmaus".

EMMAUS

"And, behold, two of them went that same day to a villge called Emmaus, which was from Jerusalem about three-score furlongs. And they talked together of all these things which had happened. And it came to pass, that, while they communed together and reasoned, Jesus himself drew near, and went with them" (Luke, XXIV 13-15). Since the Gospel description is not precise, it has never been possible to establish exactly the location of this place. The supposition which up to now has received most support identifies as the ancient village of Emmaus the place called El Qubeibeh, twelve kilometres to the North-West of Jerusalem. A large neo-Romanesque church was built there by the Franciscans in 1901. The church rises on the site once occupied by a previous religious building of the twelfth century, inside which were found the remains of an ancient house traditionally thought to be that of Cleopas, which was the setting for the scene described in St. Luke's Gospel: "And it came to pass, as he sat at meat with them, he took bread, and blessed it, and brake, and gave it to them" (Luke, XXIV 30).

Jerusalem: exterior of the Russian Cathedral of the Trinity, and the cupolas of the Russian Church of St. Mary Magdalene.

CHURCHES OF JERUSALEM

RUSSIAN CATHEDRAL OF THE TRINITY

This building, which stands out for its architectural elegance, is crowned by many green domes topped by golden crosses. It was built after the Crimean War, when it was decided to build a centre for the numerous Russian pilgrims to the Holy Land. Surrounding the Cathedral, the Russian compound contained separate hospices for male and female pilgrims, the Russian Consulate and a hospice for noble pilgrims. In front of the Cathedral lies a huge stone pillar, twelve metres long. It probably was quarried for Herod's temple but cracked and was left there.

CHURCH OF ST. MARY MAGDALENE

The architectural appearance of this church is decidedly "Muscovite", due to its seven conspicuous golden onion domes with crosses on top. The building stands in a

pleasant setting, on the western slope of the Mount of Olives and was built in 1885 by the Czar Alexander III in memory of his mother, Maria Alexandrovna. The interior houses a good number of paintings, admirable icons and the tomb of the grandduchess Elisabeth Feodorovna, killed in 1917, during the Russian Revolution.

CHURCH OF ST. MARK

The present-day building, in the Armenian Quarter of the Old City is part of a monastery complex belonging to the Syrian Orthodox Christians (Jacobites). There are vestiges of a chapel from the seventh century.

CATHEDRAL OF ST. JAMES

The centre of the Armenian Compound in the Old City, it belongs to the Orthodox Armenian Church. It is a architecturally pleasant structure whose lines are defined externally by the flow of the ogival arches. As the visitor finds it today, the building is the result of successive alterations carried out from its foundations in the eleventh century onward. It commemorates the martyrdom of the brother of John the Evangelist, James the Elder, who was decapitated in 44 A.D. by order of Herod Agrippa I. The interior is memorable for the rich texture of its decorations. It is also possible to admire three stones brought there from places sacred in the history of Israel, such as the River Jordan, Sinai and Mount Tabor.

CHURCH OF THE REDEEMER

The slender belltower of the Church of the Redeemer is given lightness by its lancet windows and crowned by a pyramidal pinnacle. Its easily recognizable outline stands out against the blue sky of the Holy City, in a quarter rich in domes and spires of various kinds. This Lutheran church was built in 1890s over the ruins of the Crusader church of Saint Mary the Latin.

◄ *Jerusalem: Church of St. Mark, exterior and interior views.*

Jerusalem: exterior views of the Cathedral of St. James, and the belltower of the Church of the Redeemer.

BASILICA OF THE DORMITION

This powerful building, dominating Mount Zion, has the imposing appearance of a fortress and is crowned by a tall, domed belltower and a conical central cupola with smaller towers at the corners. The church marks the spot where the Virgin Mary is believed to have gone to her eternal sleep, and is the last of a series of buildings which have been built there over the centuries. Erected by Kaiser Wilhelm II during the first ten years of our century, according to a design by Heinrich Renard who modelled it on the Carolingian cathedral of Aix-la-Chapelle, it belongs to the Benedictine Order. The fine circular mosaic floor and the wooden and ivory sculpture of the *Sleeping Virgin* in the crypt are worth noting.

CITY OF DAVID

CITADEL

The powerful and imposing fortifications of the Citadel are crowned by crenellated walls and towers and the distinctive cylindrical minaret improperly known as the **Tower of David**. The Citadel is the result of construction work done at the time of the Mamelukes (fourteenth century) and of later alterations during the time of Suleiman the Magnificent (first half of the sixteenth century). However, in a more ancient past, at least as far back as the time of Herod the Great, there already existed a

◄ *Jerusalem: the Basilica of the Dormition at sunset, and the Crypt with the statue of the Sleeping Virgin.*

Jerusalem: view of the Citadel dominated by the easily recognizable minaret known as the Tower of David.

Jerusalem: Tomb of David; the imposing sarcophagus is covered in a red cloth.

citadel of which interesting vestiges remain. In 24 B.C. Herod had three towers built, to which he gave the names of the people closest to him: his brother Phasael, his wife Mariamne and his friend Hippicus. In reality, these structures were the answer to the necessity for solid defense works to protect the adjoining palace. At the time of the Roman conquest, the Emperor Titus spared the towers from destruction and converted them into lodgings for the Tenth legion. The Byzantines reconstructed the fortifications, and the Muslims enlarged the Citadel. The Mamelukes expanded it in the 14th Century and the Ottomans gave it is present appearance.

The Museum of the History of Jerusalem has been set up in the interior, while the sound-and-light shows are held in the enchanted atmosphere of its fairy-tale setting.

TOMB OF DAVID

The cenotaph of King David, on the ground floor of the Mount Zion complex of buildings, is, together with the Western Wall, one of the places most visited and venerated by people of the Jewish faith. The massive, grandiose stone sarcophagus, draped in a red cloth with the star of David on it, is surmonted by twenty-two crowns of the Torah in solid silver; they represent the sovereigns who, after David, succeeded each other on the throne of Israel. (Although it has been believed since the eleventh century that this is the place where David is buried, it has also been suggested that his tomb is on Mount Ophel, near those of the other kings of Israel).

Jerusalem: The Wailing Wall stands beneath the Dome of the Rock.

Jerusalem: Jewish devotees praying at the Wailing Wall.

WAILING WALL

Called by the Jews *Hakotel Hama'aravi*, this wall is a focus of Judaism, the symbol of a people and a nation. The massive stretch of wall seen today by visitors and Jewish pilgrims from all corners of the globe, is a large segment of the sustaining wall of the Western side of the *Temple Esplanade*. The name of the wall is to be related to the Jews' long exile; the Romans prevented them from returning to their city and the Byzantines allowed them to enter it to pray, only once a year, on the anniversary of the destruction of the Temple. This custom, kept up over the centuries, became the symbol of the scattered Jewish people's hope of a return from the Exile. Between 1948 and 1967, the fact that the Wall was situated in the sector controlled by Jordan again prevented the Jews from praying there. The recovery of the Wall, after the so-called "Six-day War", was a great event, a date to be remembered in the history of the Jewish people. Among the numerous customs observed by the faithful who pray below the great, thousand-year-old, stone blocks is that of leaving in the cracks between the stones little pieces of paper with vows and prayer written on them.

Jerusalem: the remains of the Hurva Synagogue, with a big modern arch over them, and the front of the Tiferet Israël Synagogue.

Jerusalem: a view of the reconstructed cardo maximus and part of the Jewish quarter.

JEWISH QUARTER

This part of the Old City has been subjected, over the last few decades, to thorough archaeological study, so that it has been possible to reconstruct or partially restore it. The whole area was destroyed in 1948. From the thirteenth century onwards, right up to the fighting in 1948, the quarter became the home of rabbis and students at the Jewish religious seminaries, and elderly Jews who wished to die and be buried in Jerusalem.

Among the most important sights are the remains of the eighteenth century **Hurva Synagogue**, constructed over a similar building of the thirteenth century and recognizable today by a great arch restored after the destruction of the synagogue in 1948, and the **Tiferet Israel** ("Glory of Israel") **Synagogue**, which can be identified by the elegant splayed arches on the facade.

Jerusalem: The Dome of the Rock, known also as the Mosque of Omar, dominates the Temple Esplanade.

Jerusalem: Dome of the Rock, view of the interior with the rock.

TEMPLE MOUNT

At the top of the hill which has been identified as the biblical Mount Moriah spreads the *Haram es Sharif*, the great artificial esplanade which preserves the memory of the Second Temple built by Herod the Great and destroyed by the legionaries of Titus. This great space, an irregular rectangle about twelve hectares in area, is partially enclosed by powerful walled terraces. It is a universally sacred place, since it reminds Christians of two important episodes in the earthly life of Jesus; it is sacred to the Jews because they believe that the episode of Abraham and Isaac took place there, but mainly because the Temple of Solomon, and the Second Temple, stood there. At the same time it is a holy place for the Muslims, who have made it the third most important goal of pilgrimage, after

Mecca and Medina: they call it Haram es Sharif, the noble enclosure.

In the higher part, the splendid **Dome of the Rock** stands out like a jewel against the rock of Jerusalem: it was built in the second half of the seventh century by Caliph Abd El Malik. The fine majolica decorations were added by Suleiman the Magnificent (sixteenth century). Inside, a wooden railing encloses the rock which is sacred to Jews and Muslims alike. Near the southern edge of the esplanade rises the magnificent **El Aqsa Mosque**. Built by Caliph Walid (eighth century), it was enlarged by the Crusaders and changed back into a Mosque by the Moslems in 1187. The grandly monumental interior is marked by imposing columns in Carrara marble, donated by Mussolini, while the ceiling was presented by King Farouk of Egypt.

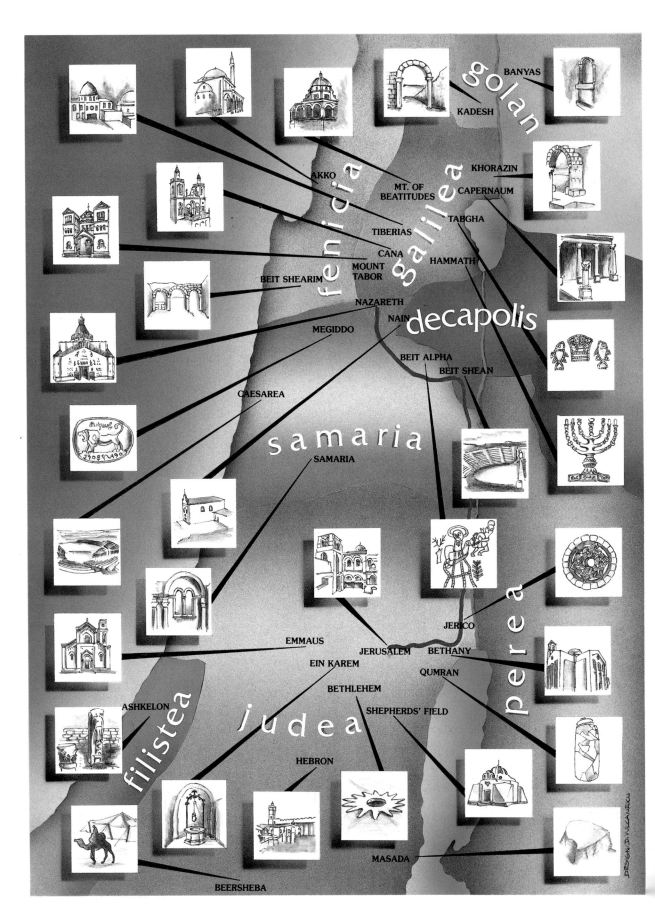

GOLAN
BANYAS
KADESH
golan

AKKO
MT. OF
BEATITUDES
fenicia
KHORAZIN
CAPERNAUM
galilea
TABGHA
TIBERIAS
CANA
HAMMATH
MOUNT
TABOR
BEIT SHEARIM
NAZARETH
NAIN
decapolis
MEGIDDO
BEIT ALPHA
BEIT SHEAN
CAESAREA

samaria
SAMARIA

JERICO

EMMAUS
JERUSALEM
BETHANY
perea
EIN KAREM
QUMRAN
BETHLEHEM
ASHKELON
SHEPHERDS' FIELD
filistea
judea
HEBRON
MASADA
BEERSHEBA

DESIGN: D. VULCANELLI

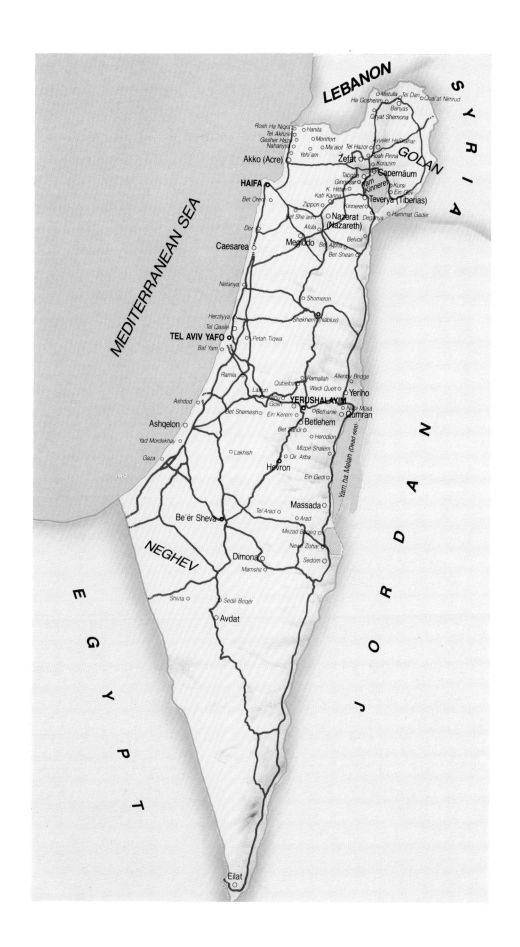

CONTENTS